The Practical Pendulum
Dan Baldwin

GW01312820

"I love the book - a very practical guide book.

"The Practical Pendulum is a must to have in your library on dowsing. It's straight forward and very easy to understand and learn. A Must for both beginners and even advanced practitioners will enjoy this book. It is also a great teaching tool for teachers."

Dave Campbell, Psychic and Medium

"I have known Dan through our connection of The Find Me group over a ten year period. We have been able to share many experiences through our Psychic work together, for which I am truly grateful.

"He shares his many Gift's and teaching's in this book about how to use a pendulum, a book I fully endorse. This is a book you will want to have. I am so pleased to have him as my friend and colleague."

Jeanette Healey, Psychic Detective

"Of all the self-help books I've read regarding tools used to enhance your own abilities, Dan's is by far the best! Easy to understand and it creates a sense of urgency and excitement to develop your own pendulum dowsing skills. I would recommend this book to all! You'll be amazed at the results!"

Rhonda Hull, Psychic Investigator

The Practical
Pendulum

getting into the swing of things

Dan Baldwin

Copyright ©2015 Dan Baldwin

All rights reserved. No part of this book may be reproduced or transmitted in any form or by any electronic or mechanical means, including photo-copying, recording or by any information storage and retrieval system currently available or yet to be devised, without the written permission of the publisher, except where permitted by law.

First Edition, June 2015
Printed in the United States of America

ISBN-13: 978-1514218105
ISBN-10: 1514218100

Also available as an electronic book in all major ebook outlets and for-mats.

Cover photo courtesy Dan Baldwin
Author photo courtesy Harvey Stanbrough
Cover layout and interior format by Debora Lewis arenapublishing.org

Dedication

"Methinks the truth should live from age to age, as 'were retailed to all posterity, even to the general all-ending day."

Shakespeare

To Dwight and Rhonda Hull, two friends whose dedication to history and truth has no limits.

Contents

What is a Pendulum? 1

What is a Pendulum Good For? 2

How Does It Work? 4

Holding the Pendulum...5

Hands Off!...6

Care and Feeding..7

My Pendulum Won't Swing...8

What If My Pendulum Swings Both Ways?...............9

My Pendulum is "Jumpy".. 10

Who Can Dowse With a Pendulum?...................... 1 1

Choosing a Pendulum.. 12

Pendulum Language 1 4

Types of Pendulums 1 5

Setting Your Pendulum 16

Think Before You Ask the Question....................... 17

As A Man Thinketh 19

Don't Focus on the Answers.................................. 20

Remain Neutral...2 1

Can I? May I? Should I? 22

An Essential Question 23

How Long Does a Session Take? 24

Listen to Your Intuition 25

Privacy 26

Pendulum Obsession 27

Health Issues 28

"Ask Your Pendulum" 29

Charts 30

Charts - Recommended Reading 31

My Ten - Step Dowsing Process 32

Step #1 – Set the Environment 32

Step #2 - Pray In 33

Step # 3 - Meditate 34

Step #4 - Psychic Protection and Clearing 34

Step #5 - Set the Intention 35

Step #6 - Ask the Questions 36

Step #7 - Remain Positive 37

Step #8 - Assume Nothing 37

Step #9 - Do The Work 38

Step #10 - Disengage 39

Map Dowsing 40

Map Dowsing – X Marks the Spot 41

Map Dowsing – Building the Box 42

A Notion on Motion 45

Dowsing in the Field 46

Dowsing Depth 49

Distance Dowsing 50

Dowsing the Human Body 51

Dowsing the Future 53

Using Your Body as a Pendulum 55

Radiesthesia 56

Stumbling Blocks 57

What if I "Lose It" and Can No Longer Get Accurate Answers? 59

Find Me 60

Exercises 61

About the Author 63

What is a Pendulum?

A pendulum is a rock on a string. Or a chunk of wood on a length of twine or a piece of metal on a chain.

That's it. There's no magic or special power in the rock, the wood, or the metal or whatever material used as the string. The pendulum is a tool, no more or less than a hammer, a can opener, car jack or a cell phone. Your pendulums should be used, respected and cared for as you would care for any valuable tool, but they should not be objects of mystery or, Heaven forbid, of worship or adoration.

My hypnotherapy instructor often referenced how some people look upon the metaphysical side of existence as seeking the "woo woo" in life. If you tag something with a funny name you can pretend you don't fear it; you don't have to face the fact that the universe is astoundingly larger then you ever thought possible. The pendulum provides a doorway into that universe, but there's no "woo woo" to be found within a rock on a string. The magic, if that's what you want to tag it, is to be found within you and your relationship to the universe.

Again, the pendulum is just an instrument for work, such as a hammer. Like a hammer, it can be used to build or it can be used to destroy. The choice is up to you.

What is a Pendulum Good For?

I'll answer a question with a question.

What do you want to know?

The information you want to know is knowable and the pendulum is one very effective tool you can use to discover that information – to make the unknown known.

Where are my missing car keys?

Is this the right job opportunity for me now?

Who is telling me the truth about this issue?

Should I see a doctor soon about this pain in my whatever?

Is the transmission giving out on my truck?

Where is the buried treasure in grandpa's north 40?

What is my probability of success in this endeavor?

Who should I see about this situation?

Which is the best product to buy?

Can I trust him/her?

When is the best time for me to do this?

You have and will always have questions and the pendulum provides a direct line to the answers you seek. For example, a close friend was considering buying a house in a nearby community. The house looked solid, was in a good neighborhood, and the purchase price was well within his budget. My friend asked me to use my pendulum to see if there were any unseen problems. I was happy to help out and so I conducted a research session on the property using my pendulum. "Is the structure sound? Does the roof leak? Is the AC system up to spec? Are there hidden problems?" I got a "yes" on that last question. A few more questions led to the swimming pool in the back yard. Later, I reported to my friend that the purchase of the house looked like a good deal, but that he should expect repair problems with the pool's cleaning system.

Within six months of buying the house, the pool cleaning system gave out. Thanks to the pendulum work, he and his wife had saved up enough funds to cover what could have been an unexpected and unpleasant repair bill.

The bottom line: if you have a question, pendulum dowsing is an effective way to determine the best answer.

How Does It Work?

The muscles in your fingers and hands move the pendulum. That movement is called an ideomotor response – an involuntary bodily movement caused by mental action – by an idea. The brain responds to the idea and the muscles respond to stimulus from the brain. But what stimulates the brain, eh?

The process involves four basic elements:

You

Your pendulum

Your subconscious mind

The higher power

The dowser (you) asks a question while holding the pendulum. It's like the hypnotist gently swinging a pocket watch before the eyes of a subject. While your conscious mind is absorbed by observation of the motion, your subconscious mind is freed up to contact the higher power. The answer comes from that higher power. Your subconscious then directs the brain which directs the muscles to move the pendulum through neuromuscular action. The pendulum swings a yes or no answer.

The process is surprisingly simple and can be learned in a short period of time. That doesn't mean it is by any means easy. Learning the basics of dowsing is not *mastering* pendulum dowsing. That requires continuing study, learning, and lots of practice.

I can't think of a better time for you to start than right now.

THE PRACTICAL PENDULUM

Holding the Pendulum

Place the string (chain, twine, thread, catgut) between your thumb and forefinger and let the weight dangle straight down so that the pendulum can swing freely. There's none of that strange "woo woo" to the technique. Just find a position that is comfortable, especially if you're planning a long session. I usually rest my elbow on my desk if I'll be working more than a few moments.

Some practitioners drape the chain over their index fingers, held in place by their thumbs, to do the work. Give the different positions a good try and determine which hold is best for you.

I keep my wrist straight rather than bent or sagging. Again, there's nothing mystical about the position. I just want to keep the blood flow natural while working and I don't want muscle fatigue to set in and affect the motion of the pendulum.

Sometimes a desk or table isn't available during some of my pendulum work – searching for a missing person or object in the outdoors, for example. In those cases I hold out my left palm open (I am right handed) and dangle the pendulum directly over it. Some dowsers say this technique is powerful anytime because it reflect the energy back to the pendulum and the pendulum operator.

Experiment with variations on the basic hold if you want. Use a technique that is comfortable and one in which you feel confident. Again, whatever works for you is what's best for you and your work.

Hands Off!

You should be the only person to handle your pendulum. Some say this is a "guy thing" in that you just don't loan out your tools. Others note that we live in a universe of vibration – vibes. Your vibes become in tune with your pendulum through repeated use. When someone else – a different set of vibes – uses your pendulum, those vibrations are affected which in turn affects any future readings you may do.

I was once excoriated in an e-mail blast from a participant in one of my Practical Pendulum classes in which I had allowed the participants to handle one of my pendulums. The e-mailer was shocked and outraged at such a display of carelessness on my part. Had she invested the time to speak with me, she would have learned that I have a "demo" pendulum used solely for demonstrations and classes. Any participant is welcome to use that one pendulum and I never use that one for any of my work.

As for the rest of my collection, it's strictly hands off.

I don't need any more bad vibes.

Care and Feeding

I keep my pendulums on several small sheets of selenite, a translucent crystal form of gypsum. It is also known as Maria Glass, Satin Spar, and Desert Rose. The theory is that selenite cleanses the pendulums of any negative vibes or energy blocks that have been picked up during a dowsing section.

For the scientific minded reader, selenite is a variety of gypsum, a soft mineral that can be scratched by the human fingernail.

For the metaphysical reader, selenite is said to be a protective stone which helps connect us to our guardians, guides, and Higher Self.

The ancients believed certain crystals waxed and waned with the moon and the word is derived from the Latin *selenites* which means moonstone or stone of the moon. Selene is the Greek goddess of the moon, sister of the sun god Helios.

Mythology aside, I recommend that you keep your pendulums on selenite. Whether you're of a scientific or metaphysical nature, if nothing else, the mineral will brighten up your office and, when guests ask about it, give you an opportunity to show off you knowledge of ancient religious practices.

Selenite is available in rock and mineral stores and psychic bookshops and is an inexpensive purchase.

My Pendulum Won't Swing

Yes, it will.

Just be patient and give the process time to work. Don't let a seemingly dead pendulum discourage you from dowsing, especially if you are just beginning. Sometimes my pendulum swings wildly and sometimes the motion is barely detectible. The amount of motion, the size of the swing, isn't relevant. A "yes" is a "yes" and a "no" is a "no" regardless of the circumference of the circle above your desk, map, hand or chart.

It is perfectly acceptable to jump start your pendulum with a back-and-forth swing just to get things moving. Don't start it spinning in either a yes or a no direction, which could affect your concentration and therefore your answer. Just get it in motion and then proceed.

You can also think or speak "spin wider" if you want a more powerful swing. The important thing is to allow your subconscious to direct this effort.

What If My Pendulum Swings Both Ways?

That's quite common when beginning a session. You'll can get a series of yes-no-yes-no answers before the pendulum settles down. Don't let this throw you. Just focus on your question and allow the system to work. And it will work. The correct swing will occur and you will have your answer.

The more you work with pendulums the better you will be at feeling and understanding what is going on during the process. You will soon know when you and your subconscious are working and when you're just warming up for the session.

My Pendulum is "Jumpy"

I gave a pendulum to a close friend who was interested in learning the process, but he backed away when the "jumpy" motions of the pendulum frightened him. He said his pendulum actually jumped up and down on its string before he could begin. If this or something similar happens, don't panic. It's just a sign that things are all lined up and you're rarin' to go. Your mind, body, spirit, pendulum and the higher power are all attuned and it's time to put all those strengths to work. A lot of energy is present and it needs to be released. Don't fear it; use it. Release all that pent up power by doing good work with your pendulum.

Who Can Dowse With a Pendulum?

Anyone.

Pendulum is not a gift for the special or the anointed few. As with any skill, different people will have different levels of success, but there's no secret password needed to join the club. All you need is:

Belief that it works

Belief that you can do it

Practice

Application of techniques

Concentration

Take note that your physical, mental or emotional state can have an effect, sometimes a powerful effect, on how *well* you dowse. If you've had a couple of shots of your favorite adult beverage, your accuracy with the pendulum will be affected – just as your ability to drive would be affected. You might not notice it – "I'm fine, officer" – but the negative effect is there. The same holds for dowsing while on some prescription medications. A dowser suffering from a severe case of the flu will not be as accurate as when he or she is healthy. A fight with your boss or spouse or an unpleasant encounter that puts you in a foul mood will probably foul up your reading. Whatever effects your life in any area can affect your performance with the pendulum. Adjust your pendulum work schedule accordingly.

Part of the discipline of dowsing, is to make sure the conditions are right for a successful reading. Another part of the discipline is in knowing when it's better to hold off the session until the situation is more conducive to success.

Choosing a Pendulum

There's no science to choosing a pendulum; just pick one that you like. I look through the selection for the one that shouts "Take me home, Dan. Take me home." That's intuition at work. Intrinsically, there's no one pendulum better than any other pendulum, so just look through a lineup of pendulums and pick up the one that appeals to you. Trust your instincts by allowing your subconscious to make the decision. If one catches your eye because you're attracted to the pretty color, the type of material, or the shape, then that's reason enough.

Most of mine are elongated diamond shapes made of stone and most of those stones are some form of crystal. My choice is determined by practical and aesthetic means. I do a lot of map dowsing, so the pointed tip of my favorite shape is helpful in pinpointing specific locations. The size of a pendulum tip can represent the size of a football field on a "topo," so the sharper the point, the better for my purposes. The heavy weight of the pendulum is also helpful when dowsing outdoors where the wind can easily affect the movement.

Aesthetically, I like the look, color and feel of polished stone, so that's why I choose pendulums fitting that description.

Again, there's no science involved; no magic either.

Experiment with different shapes, materials, sizes and weights. You'll eventually find what works best.

The length of the string is a matter of personal preference. I have short and long string pendulums, but my preference is for strings of 10 – 15 inches in length. The reason is just that I am comfortable using that length. Whatever distance works best

THE PRACTICAL PENDULUM

for you is the right length.

Watch out for pendulum obsession when buying (or making your own) pendulum. Don't get caught up in over-thinking the process of making a selection. After all, it's only a rock on a string.

Pendulum Language

Pendulum motions are basic:
Circle right
Circle left
Left-to-Right
Front-to-Back
Nine times out of ten a circle right is a "yes" answer. Circle left is a "no" answer. A left-to-right or front-to-back motion means you need to rephrase the question. This is a general rule that holds most of the time. There are exceptions, so refer to the *Setting Your Pendulum* chapter that follows for more details.

There's no way your subconscious can provide an either/or answer to a multiple choice question. For example, "Are my missing car keys in the kitchen or the living room?" It's impossible to get an answer to that question using a pendulum because the question isn't a yes/no question. You will need to be more specific to dowse a correct answer.

"Are my missing car keys in the kitchen?"

"Are my missing keys in the living room?"

"Are my missing keys behind the couch in the living room?"

"Are my missing keys under the cat behind the couch in my living room?"

As with any area of research, the key to getting a good answer is to ask good questions.

Naturally this yes/no format lends itself to getting directions. "Are my missing car keys north of the kitchen?" I will cover this in the section on map dowsing.

Types of Pendulums

One type, the most commonly used, is a solid weight on a string. The weight can be of any material heavy enough so that the force of gravity can be employed. Most of my pendulums are made of various types of rock, but that's just because that's what I prefer. I also have pendulums of wood, metal and artificial materials.

The second type is hollow and it works on the theory of "sympathetic resonance." That's a fancy way of saying use the substance you're seeking to find the substance you're seeking. If you're dodging Texas size rattlesnakes in the Permian Basin looking for a spot to plant a new oil well, you would fill the empty space with oil. It's an application of "like attracts like." The substance put into the hollow pendulum is called the "witness." Why it's called that, I do not know. I guess "witness" sounds better than "stuff."

A word of caution when using sympathetic resonance – the substance you put into the pendulum is the substance that will attract the pendulum. So, if you're looking for that new oil well, but you take the short cut of putting motor oil, or 3-In-One oil, or sludge from under your auto dealer's service rack into the witness, that's what will attract the pendulum and that's what you will find.

Setting Your Pendulum

The pendulum swings left and right, back and forth, and in a circling motion right or left in response to your questions. Setting your pendulum is just a way of aligning yourself with your pendulum and the process so that you recognize those answers each time you dowse. You're not *commanding* the rock or metal or material to do anything; it's an inanimate object. Basically, you're just putting you, your instrument and your higher self on the same wavelength.

In most cases, a circular swing to the right corresponds to a "yes" and a circular swing to the left corresponds to a "no." I have encountered a very few cases in which the opposite is true.

A swing back and forth or left and right means that you have asked a question in a way that cannot be answered with a yes or a no. Ask the question again.

When you get a new pendulum set it by saying or thinking, "Show me the movement for a 'yes' answer." Repeat the process by saying, "Show me the movement for a 'no' answer." Also ask, "Show me the motion for "Ask the question another way."

I go through this process with every pendulum I acquire.

Think Before You Ask the Question

Poorly worded questions produce poor answers. Think and think carefully about the words you use to formulate a question and especially about what those words mean to you.

For example, in my work for Find Me (see the Find Me section of this book), I use pendulum dowsing to locate missing persons and to help the authorities solve crimes. In looking for a missing person it's important to determine whether that person is alive, injured, disabled or deceased. That's a basic starting point for all the questions that have to follow in locating that person or that person's human remains.

I used to ask, "Is this missing person alive?" I would always get a "yes" answer and would then proceed with my research based on that information. Many times, the person had crossed over before I even began my initial reading. How could I be so wrong so many times about so important a subject, I wondered.

One day the light bulb over my head flickered on and I figured it out.

I believe in the immortality of the soul. Even though a person's human body may be lifeless, that person's soul continues. The person represented by that soul is very much alive, so, of course, I was getting "yes" answers. The body was dead, but the person continued living in a different form.

The question I now use is, "Is this missing person *physically* alive...."

Some psychics extend the question. "Is this missing person physically alive on this planet in this universe and this dimension and at this time?"

The important matter to take away from this chapter is that

you must interpret your answers in context with your personal beliefs and world view, which inevitably affect your dowsing.

As A Man Thinketh

Your pendulum reacts to the question in your mind, not the one on your lips. Focus on the question and keep your mind focused on that question throughout the process or you will get inaccurate answers. Successful dowsing requires that you focus exclusively on the problem at hand.

If your mind wanders, your subconscious and therefore your pendulum motions will wander with it. Let's say that you ask, "Are my car keys in the living room?" But your mind wanders and you start thinking, "Should I put more cumin in my chili for supper tonight?" You'll get the correct answer, but that answer will reflect the dietary nature of your thought processes and not the needs for reliable transportation.

Don't Focus on the Answers

Focusing on the answer leads to producing the desired-for answer and not necessarily the true answer.

For example, "Do I have a serious illness?"

When you focus on the answer your thought processes follow this pattern. "Do I have a serious illness ...do I have a serious illness...a serious illness... serious illness... I have a serious illness... serious illness... serious illness...." I have run into this problem when searching for missing persons. "Is the little girl alive...is she alive...she is alive...alive...alive...alive..." Because the mind wants what the heart wants, the pendulum process provides the answer the heart commands. Obviously, that's not always the right answer.

One technique to avoid this trap is to continually ask the question while working your pendulum. Some people continually run a neutral thought through their minds or provide a command. "Correct answer...correct answer...correct answer...." Others think or recite their mantra until the answer is provided. It is important that you do not allow your conscious mind to direct the process. Let the subconscious take and maintain control

Remain Neutral

A follow up to the previous chapter is important. Emotions affect dowsing. A dowser must not allow emotions into the process and that can be a significant challenge. Assuming the desired answer will probably produce the desired answer, which may not be the correct answer. I face this constantly in my work looking for missing persons. When I ask, "Is the beautiful little five year old girl physically alive?" I desperately want that little girl to be alive. My heart cries out for the girl and her family, so naturally my emotions lean toward a happy outcome. Those emotions can and in most cases will lead to inaccurate answers. Inaccurate answers can't help find missing persons, bring criminals to justice, bring closure to a family, or solve any problem you may face.

You must find a way to remain neutral while dowsing regardless of the emotional charges in and around you. Place your dowsing mind in a separate place, or "box," from your emotions while dowsing. It helps me to think of the subject, whether or not a person, as just that – a subject – while dowsing.

While working, keep the emotions in neutral gear. There is always time for tears or cheers after you've done the work. Follow your heart, your fears or your desires and your emotions, not your higher self will be your guide. As challenging as it may be, keep your emotions under control. Focus on the process and you will get the correct answers.

Ultimately, isn't that what your heart really desires?

Can I? May I? Should I?

These are three questions dowsers ask before practicing their craft. They are especially important when doing serious work, such as locating a missing person or tracking down a suspected murderer.

Can I do this work?

May I do this work?

Should I do this work?

After you've mastered the craft you will get a feel for the answers to these questions without having to ask them.

I worked a missing child case many years ago in which I did not ask these questions up front. After doing my pendulum dowsing I was honing in on a location for the missing little girl (a process described elsewhere in this book) and I knew that I was getting close. My work had narrowed the search area to a specific small town in the rural part of a southwestern state. But I developed an uncomfortable feeling about the project and the closer I got to the little girl's location, the more uncomfortable I became. I finally ask the three questions and got a strong "no" on the "should I" question.

I dropped the case and notified the people I was working with, explaining that I felt it was not in the girl's best interest for me to continue. Later on, facts came to light that proved the validity of asking those questions. It seems that the relatives of the missing girl weren't interested in her wellbeing at all, but they were very interested in the money she stood to inherit. In other words, it was not in the missing person's best interest to be found by those people at that time.

An Essential Question

When dowsing important matters, especially those involving interaction with other people, it's a good idea to ask the following question:

"Is this action (new job/partner/opportunity) for the highest good?"

How Long Does a Session Take?

The answers to your questions are immediate. After all, you're just asking yes/no or up/down or now/later type questions. If the challenge is simple, the process may take only a minute or so.

If the matter is important, conduct multiple readings over an extended timeframe if possible. For example, a request to locate a missing person usually comes in with a deadline. That deadline permitting, I like to conduct an initial reading immediately, a second reading midway through and then another just before submitting my report at the deadline.

"How long" depends on many factors, but after working with your pendulum for a while, you will develop a sense of exactly what those words mean and the length of time you need to plan for the work.

Listen to Your Intuition

The only limits on your dowsing ability are those you place on yourself. Your belief affects your performance. As you practice and develop your dowsing skills you will become more attuned to what will and what will not work and what you should and should not dowse.

Don't limit developing your intuition to just the time invested in dowsing. Train your mind to respond immediately to your intuitive thoughts as they arrive. When driving down the interstate and you get a feeling that you should immediately change lanes, do so. (Check your mirrors first!) If you get an impression that you should take the stairs instead of the elevator, act on it. When reaching for a red shirt and your mind says wear the blue, grab the hanger with the blue shirt.

It's unlikely that any of these actions will fall into the earth-shattering, life-changing category. But 18-wheelers do seemingly come out of nowhere. Elevators do get stuck and people get trapped in them for many unpleasant hours. Spiders do hide in shirt collars. The goal is to train your mind to respond immediately to intuitive thoughts. Your dowsing will benefit from those exercises – as will other aspects of your life.

Privacy

Pendulum dowsing is not limited by time or space, but its use should always be defined by the rules of decency. If the subject is none of your business, then it is none of your business and you should direct your efforts to more positive pursuits.

Pendulum Obsession

The talented woman who manages to shear my scalp once a month told me she had recently gone to the grocery store where she encountered a woman dowsing a loaf of bread with a pendulum.

This is the kind of activity that gives pendulum dowsing a bad name.

Pendulum dowsing is a great tool with unlimited capabilities, but you can carry anything too far. Unless that loaf of bread was slightly green and was placed in the Very Much Older Than Day-Old Bread bin, the woman was obsessing with her pendulum. That's not smart. It's not necessary. And it's not healthy.

Health Issues

Dowsing health issues is easy, especially when using charts listing illnesses, conditions, remedies and so on. As an *initial step* this is okay, but follow up with a visit with your doctor or medical provider.

Do not depend solely on pendulum dowsing for answers to medical and health issues for you or your loved ones. For one thing you are far too close to *you*. Confidence in a process flawed by your desires or fears can have serious health consequences. The chances of getting inaccurate answers based on emotional reactions to questions rather than accurate answers based on proper technique is extreme. That's especially true when the patient is you or someone with whom you have an emotional bond.

Also, some people enjoy being sick. That sounds contradictory, but search your memory banks and you'll find someone you know who is happiest when miserable. That attitude can affect a reading, too.

The bottom line: dowse, but see your physician before prescribing any remedy.

"Ask Your Pendulum."

I often answer with this phrase when someone asks me about a question related to some aspect of his or her life.

You'll hear and/or read it a lot when doing some of your pendulum homework.

"Isn't this a contradiction with your statement that there is no magic in a pendulum," you ask.

Yes, it is a contradiction, but it is also acceptable shorthand. You haven't caught the author in a gotcha moment. "Ask your pendulum" is just easier to say and write then "consult with your higher power using the pendulum of your choice with proper dowsing technique under appropriate conditions with adequate focus on the subject at hand."

Charts

Pendulum dowsing is a slow process when researching any complex subject. The yes/no nature of the answers assures this. The process can be exhausting. You can shortcut a significant amount of labor and time through the use of pendulum charts.

For example, let's assume you are dowsing for a name and that name is Joe. You begin with, "Is the first letter of the first name the letter A?" The answer is no, so you continue asking the same question ten times until you get 'yes' on the letter J. Now you start all over again. "Is the second letter of the first name the letter A?" Fifteen swings later, you finally get a 'yes' on the letter O. and five swings later you finally get the full first name with an E. Imagine if the name you're trying to dowse is newsman James Allen Miklaszewski.

An alphabet chart arranges the 26 letters in a circle. Sometimes the numbers 0 to 9 are included. To use the chart, you just hold the pendulum over the center of the circle and ask the question, "What is the first letter of the first name?" The pendulum swings to the letter J and then you move on. You discover the full name in a fraction of the time it takes to dowse the name letter-by-letter from A to Z.

Charts cover an incredibly wide range of subjects. A partial list from one book, which lists 50 charts, includes: probability, percentages, yes/no, herbal remedies, relationships, house, business, chakras, glands, medications, gemstones, chakras, personal motivators, vitamins, and even "how to change my life."

The amount of time and effort using pendulum charts saves is immense and I strongly urge you to acquire them.

Charts – Recommended Reading

I highly recommend *The Pendulum Charts – The Doorway To Knowing Your Intuitive Mind* by Dale W. Olsen.

If you only purchase one pendulum book (after mine, of course), this is the one to get.

My Ten - Step Dowsing Process

I developed this process after studying a number of books, consulting other dowsers, and experiencing a lot of trial and error. As with the rock on a swing, there's no magic in the formula; it's just a process that works. The ten steps are a good way to get started. After mastering them, you can adapt them to whatever process works best for you.

Step #1 - Set the Environment

The more peaceful and quiet your environment, the better. I close the blinds in my office and use only a single table lamp for illumination. I place the light directly over my pendulum, notebook, charts, maps or whatever I may be using at the time. I light a scented candle for a while. I also play very low key New Age music or war "white noise" headphones at a very low volume throughout the process.

None of this setting the environment has anything at all to do with the "woo woo" factor. There's no magic or symbolism involved. The process isn't a ceremony. Like an athlete stretching before an event, it's just a warm up.

I dim the lights, play the music, and light the candle just to block as much of the outside world interference as possible. If the lights were up, I could easily be distracted by a sudden glance at a book cover or a photograph hanging on my wall. If the blinds were open, I could lose concentration when a neighbor walks by, a bird lands in the tree across the street, or when anything interesting happens on the other side of the glass. The music helps drown out street noise, planes landing in the nearby airport, and the practice sessions of "Eight Guys With Banjos with Gus on Tuba" practicing in the garage next door.

The fewer distractions you have, the better your chances of a successful session.

Step #2 - Pray In

Regardless of your religious beliefs and practices or lack of them, it is essential that you pray in. Those who have religious beliefs know who to talk to: God, Goddess, Gaia, the universe, the ancestors, or The Great Big Nice Pink Something In The Sky. Pray in to the Higher Power, however you may view that power. If you're agnostic, a disbeliever in Higher Powers, or just uncomfortable with the whole concept, pray in to your Higher Self or to your subconscious mind.

Why pray in?

Because the act aligns you with the positive forces that allow you to do good work. It is a recognition that you are a part of something bigger than yourself and a willing participant in the process of making that something bigger something better.

What should I pray?

The wording is completely up to you, but the core message should be a request that you do good work. It's that simple. You don't need to be elaborate. "I am one with the Father (Universe/God/All). The Father and I are one" is a good place to start.

One of the best prayers along this line was uttered by astronaut Alan Shepard as he was about to become America's first man in space. "Oh, Lord, please don't let me f--- up." If you think about that, it's a pretty damn good prayer for dowsing.

Keep it short and to the point. There's no reason to build a ceremony around praying in.

Just do it and move on to the next step.

Step # 3 - Meditate

Ten to twenty minutes of quiet meditation helps calm the mind and relax the body so that you can concentrate on the upcoming work. Occasionally, I meditate on the subject I am about to dowse, but that is rare. It's a bit of putting the cart before the horse. Generally, I just meditate on relaxation and connecting with my higher self.

You can find lots of good books or go online to find meditation techniques. You can find classes on the subject in most communities, so I won't get into the techniques in these pages. All you need to know is readily available from many sources. I urge you to take full advantage of them.

Meditation is a wonderful technique for all kinds of things, but don't get caught up in the process when preparing to dowse. Your goal isn't to have a metaphysical experience, but just to relax and get into alignment. Meditate and then move on.

Step #4 - Psychic Protection and Clearing

Again, without getting metaphysical on you, it's important to recognize that there are negative forces at work in the universe. How you define those forces is, to me, irrelevant. The important matter is that you recognize their existence and take appropriate steps to protect yourself from them while doing pendulum work.

How you engage in psychic protection is a personal and private matter. What counts is that you do it.

I prefer the proven standby of visualizing myself surrounded by a sphere of pure white light through which no negative forces can enter. A line borrowed from psychic John Edward reinforces that image, "I am surrounded by the pure white light of God's divine and protective love." Psychic protection can be that fast and that simple.

Whatever image works best for you is what works best for you. Some people visualize themselves within a fortress, a battleship or an armored tank. At the other end of the spectrum some people visualize themselves in an entirely different yet safe environment, such as mom's kitchen where cookies are baking and everything is safe and secure.

I hike alone in an Arizona desert in areas inhabited by rattlesnakes, bear, javelina, mountain lions and other critters who would love to have me over for dinner. I would never go on a wilderness trek without my pistol, knife and cell phone – not because I go looking for trouble, but because I know trouble is out there and I want to do all I can to avoid it.

I also clear my work area of negative forces, blocks and interferences. After praying in, I simply ask that those negative forces, blocks and interferences be removed and taken to the appropriate place of healing and clearing.

It's the psychic equivalent of clearing off your desk to begin work.

Step #5 - Set the Intention

Focus is essential for all pendulum work and stating your

intention in clear language is essential to effective dowsing.

Praying in is not setting your intention. "Oh, Lord, please don't let me foul up" is not the same as "My goal is to find a reliable water source on the north 40."

Set your intention in specific language and without ornamentation.

"My intention is to find my missing car keys this morning."

"My intention is to locate missing person John Doe."

"My intention is to discover my life's purpose."

Before you begin, think about your intention. Boil down the meaning into a few meaningful words and state it clearly. The more complex the question, the more challenging the process in getting the answers. Remember that famous KISS rule. Keep It Simple, Stupid. Then, get to work.

Step #6 - Ask the Questions

This is where you ask those questions mentioned earlier:

"Can I?"

"May I?"

"Should I?"

I suggest two additional questions to ask before you begin work?

"Will I Get Accurate Answers Now?"

If the answer is "no," consider putting off the session until a later time if possible. Any number of reasons could be interfering with your research. The Universe (however you choose to define that) may have determined that the time is not right. You may have a bad head cold. Pressure at work may be affecting your ability to concentrate. The city could be about to move heavy construction machinery in front of your home to start using brain-numbing noisy machinery digging up the utility lines.

If you're not going to get accurate answers, what is the point of dowsing at this time?

Note that you can dowse the reason for the inaccuracy and that you may be able to use your pendulum to remove that block or interference and then start dowsing knowing you will get accurate answers.

"Is dowsing for this answer for the highest good?"

Sometimes the greatest good is served by not dowsing and moving on to something else.

Step #7 - Remain Positive

Dowsing is slow, often tedious work and it's easy to become ground down by the process. Even the best and most experienced dowsers have to work hard at getting consistently accurate answers. It is essential that you remain positive throughout the process. Remember that the techniques have been proven for thousands of years by practitioners throughout the world.

Pendulum dowsing works.

Remember also, that you know the process and that you're doing good work. The answers are out there and are available. Never doubt. You're good and you'll get better.

Step #8 - Assume Nothing

The only thing blocking the pathway from the Higher Power to your subconscious to the finger muscles that move your pendulum is your conscious mind. Assuming the answer, even if that answer appears to be blatantly obvious, affects the quality of your dowsing – usually in a negative manner. Try as best you can to avoid thinking about the answer before and during your process.

I heard a police report of an elderly man who went missing in my neighborhood. There is an undeveloped desert area near where he was last seen so I "just knew" where he could be found. I did a pendulum reading, which confirmed my assumption so I immediately grabbed my water bottle, put on my hiking boots and invested the afternoon scouring that area. I found nothing. The hundreds of people who later turned out and searched the neighborhood, including my target area, found nothing. That was several years ago. The man is still missing.

I wonder now that if I had slowed down and followed my own process rather than letting my assumption rule my judgment if I would have dowsed the correct location. I'll never know.

The only thing to assume is that you are a blank page. Pendulum dowsing, done correctly, will provide the writing and the appropriate message on that page.

Step #9 - Do The Work

Once you've covered the preceding steps, you're ready to start dowsing.

Ask the question.

Get to work.

If you're dowsing something significant, such as the location of a missing person, realize that you may have to conduct several sessions to arrive at the correct answer. Different sessions may produce different results. You may get "yes" one day and on the same question get a "no" in another session. That's just the way things sometimes work. We have good days and bad days. Look at all the work sessions over whatever time period you have been working and then make your evaluation.

"Which session or sessions have come up with the correct answer," you ask? My answer is, "Ask your pendulum." Verify the accuracy of your dowsing report by asking about that accuracy. This is where those percentage charts come in handy. I shoot for 95 percent accuracy or higher. The charts will help you evaluate which of the readings are accurate or are most accurate.

Also recommended: I verify my accuracy periodically throughout each session. When the accuracy starts dropping, that's an indication that it's probably time to give things a rest.

Step #10 - Disengage

At the end of a session I make a conscious effort to disengage from the process. Simply state, "I disengage from this process (session/effort) now." I have trained my mind so that I just think the word *disengage* at the end of a session and that's it.

It's important because you don't want to carry around any psychic baggage picked up during the session. You've done good work, now let it go and get on with the rest of the day's labors.

Map Dowsing

Dowsing is not limited by distance. If you can dowse the location of your missing car keys on one room of your house (and you can), you can just as easily dowse the location of a missing person on the other side of the city, state or country.

For example, the psychic detecting group I belong to, Find Me, was asked by the local authorities in a Colorado county to help locate the human remains of a missing person, a victim of suspected foul play. I used map dowsing techniques and located two GPS coordinates on a specific mountain north of Durango. Others in the group had similar results. Later investigations revealed that the authorities were certain that one of my dowsed locations was a crime scene. On-site searchers also discovered human remains 300 ft. from my other GPS location. The remains were identified by DNA as those of the victim. Note that the tip of a pendulum held over a map can represent an area the size of a football field or larger. Also, note that the GPS locations were more than 350 miles from where I dowsed those locations and in places I had never seen, been to or heard of. I do not brag; any dowser can obtain the same quality of results. A room, a city a world – to a pendulum dowser distance is irrelevant.

The process is simple: (1) Get a map and (2) start dowsing.

Map Dowsing
X Marks the Spot

A map can be your world atlas, a roadmap, topological map, or even an empty square drawn on a sheet of paper.

You can place a pointer (such as a pencil tip) on the map and ask the yes/no question, "Is the missing person or item here?" Obviously, the larger the map the bigger the challenge and the bigger investment in research time. You can use more efficient techniques.

One is the "X marks the spot" technique. Take a straight line, such as a ruler, and place in an east/west alignment and move it north or south from one edge of the map to the other – top to bottom or bottom to top. Swing your pendulum and ask for a "yes" response when the ruler reaches the east/west axis of the missing subject. Draw the line. Repeat the process with the ruler in a north/south alignment moving it east or west on the map. Again, ask for a "yes" response when you reach the north/south axis. Draw the line.

The point where the lines intersect is the point where the missing subject is located. X really does mark the spot.

Two people can do this together. One moves the ruler while the other swings the pendulum. Be aware that one of the operators could affect the other's performance without realizing it. A look, a gesture, a cough, or even a change in breathing patterns could affect the outcome. It's a good idea to work this process blind with the dowser and the person with the map doing the process back to back or separated by some distance.

Map Dowsing
Building the Box

I call the technique I use most often "building the box." I begin by creating a box defined by north/south and east/west boundaries. For example, if I was to dowse for something in Arizona my northern boundary would be the Arizona-Utah state line; the southern boundary the Arizona-Mexico border; the eastern boundary would be the Arizona-New Mexico state line; and the western boundary would be the Arizona-California/Nevada state line. That's the box. The same guidelines apply to a nation, a city, a house, a room and so on.

The next step is to reduce the size of the box to a specific GPS point. The goal is to reduce the search area from the universe to the size of a dot.

I'd do this by asking a series of questions designed to shrink the search area.

"Is the missing subject north of I-40?"

"Is the missing subject east of I-17?"

"Is the missing subject north of I-10?"

Let's assume the answer is yes to all three. In a matter of less than a minute, I have reduced the size of the search area from the entire State of Arizona to approximately one quarter of the state. Further questions reduce the size of the box even more.

"Is the missing subject north of Hwy. 70?"

"Is the missing subject south of Hwy. 60/77?"

"Is the missing subject west of Hwy. 191?"

Again, let's assume the answers are yes to all three questions. Now, the search area is reduced to Graham County, AZ.

THE PRACTICAL PENDULUM

That's much better, but still too big an area for a Search and Rescue or Search and Recovery.

At this point, I like to start using a book of topological maps of the state. These are available for all states in map shops and bookstores everywhere. Map shops can also provide individual topological maps of specific geographical areas. "Topos" are very detailed maps showing virtually everything in a given area: terrain, elevations, urban and rural areas, roads, backroads, trails, land features, windmills, mines, dams and so on.

Using my Arizona Atlas & Gazetteer, my topo book, I can see that Graham County is represented by map areas designated 54, 55, 62 and 63. A yes/no question determines that the missing subject is in area 54. We already know that the subject is south of Hwy. 60, which runs through the 54 block, so the box has now been reduced a triangle roughly 30 miles by 15 miles by 15 miles.

At this point, I can begin using my pointer to zoom in on the location. More yes/no questions follow. Is the missing subject north/south/east/west of a specific town? Is it N/S/E/W of a specific road? Is it N/S/E/W of a specific land feature, such as a mine or a lake? By continuing to ask questions, I continue to shrink the size of the box to a pinpointed location. In this scenario, let's assume your topo research has brought you to the town of Bylas, Az.

That's pretty good, but you can get even closer, down to specific GPS coordinates, by logging on to Google Earth. I type in the search area and within seconds zoom in to an aerial view of the area showing roads, rooftops, yards, playgrounds, buildings, trees and shrubs. More yes/no questions shrink the box further. At this level I can use a pointer, such as a pencil tip, to indicated very specific locations. "Is the missing subject in this house? In this building? In this plowed field? In this back yard?" Google Earth will provide the image and the GPS coordinates. Let's say your search indicates that the missing subject is located on the Gila River bridge just north of town. At the bottom of the Google Earth screen you'll see a series of numbers. In this case the GPS coordinates for the middle of that bridge are 33 09 53.14N and 110 08 02.51 W. That's your X that marks the spot.

Through a process of elimination, your pendulum dowsing has reduced the search area from the entire State of Arizona to a specific area which can be covered on location by your right foot.

A Notion on Motion

I worked on a Find Me case many years ago in which I dowsed the location of a missing person as being in the area of east Phoenix. Another psychic indicated a location in west Phoenix. Others pinpointed specific locations in western Arizona and eastern California. The missing person was found a few weeks later in San Francisco. (He was found by family members who followed directions from several other Find Me members.)

I wondered how I and the others working that case could be so far off. Later, I was able to review the case files and I noticed something interesting. My east Phoenix location was on a Tuesday. The west Phoenix location was dated the following day. The western Arizona and eastern California locations were days later and days apart. It turns out that the psychics' locations were not wrong after all. *They were correct for the day of the individual reading.*

The point: if you're dowsing for something that could be in motion, such as a human being, allow for that motion in your readings. Instead of being wrong, your sessions could be creating a direct line to the subject.

Dowsing in the Field

Most of my pendulum dowsing is done within my office, but occasionally I have used dowsing techniques in the field. Here's an example of an exercise I took that demonstrates the process.

I recommend using a pendulum with some weight to it as wind will be a factor when working out of doors.

I am a history buff and I enjoy hiking to areas where events happened. I combined my interest in history with my desire to practice dowsing in the field by trying an exercise out in the desert of Arizona. The challenge was to find an ancient, Native American artifact (any artifact) within half mile square test area. The artifact was just a target; I didn't have anything specific in mind. I could have used targets such as mining equipment, U.S. Cavalry buttons, cowboy artifacts – this was just a training exercise.

The first question was basic. "Is there an ancient Native American artifact within the target area that I can find today?" Notice the qualifiers "within the target area" and "today."

The next course was to find a direction: north, south, east or west. I honed in on the true direction by asking the pendulum to point the way. In this case, the pendulum moved in a northeast/southwest direction. Instinct told me that the subject would be found in the northeasterly direction and not the southwestern. As you work with your pendulum, you will also get a good feel for such things. In the meantime, just ask. "Is the direction I should follow to the northeast?"

THE PRACTICAL PENDULUM

I was conducting this exercise without a map, but if I had brought along a topo, the line I had dowsed would have been drawn on the map as an aid in the search.

I then determined the approximate distance. "Is the artifact within half a mile? A quarter of a mile? Three hundred yards. One hundred yards? I continued this process, getting "yes" answers until I got a "no" at the question, "Is the artifact within fifty yards?" At that point I knew what I was looking for was within 50 – 75 yards north/northeast of where I was standing. Additional questions narrowed the distance to 60 yards.

I paced off 60 yards and asked, "Am I within 15 feet of the target?" Again, I asked a series of qualifying questions until I got 10 feet, which I then paced off ending up in a desert wash. If my dowsing was accurate, I was standing near, or perhaps even on, the target object. But, I could see nothing other than sand and rocks.

"Which direction should I look to find the artifact?" The answer was "right." I looked down and to my right, but could only see a fairly large, flat rock. "Is the artifact under that rock?" I got a "no" response. "Is the artifact buried?" Again, "no." The artifact wasn't hanging from a tree, so in desperation I turned over the rock.

The rock was the artifact – an overturned U-shaped grinding stone 700 years old or older. Pendulum dowsing had led me to within less than a footstep of the target.

Dowsing in the field is just like map dowsing at home, except that you have the benefit of being in a position to ask more detailed questions. "Is the target behind that oak tree? Buried beneath that shed? Hidden within this cave?" "Is it physically safe to enter this abandoned building?"

You can practice this technique in your neighborhood park. Get a friend to hide or to hide something in the field and then go find it/him/her using your pendulum. This form of "hide 'n seek" is a great way to build up your dowsing skills.

THE PRACTICAL PENDULUM

Dowsing Depth

Whether seeking the proper depth to plant a shrub or the amount of digging necessary to bring to light the gold from the Lost Dutchman Mine, the dowsing technique is the same as for any other research. Just use your yes/no questions to find an area and then build and shrink the box around the target location. The only difference is that you'll be working on a vertical instead of a horizontal plane.

When seeking depth or height, make sure that you first determine the measurement to be used.

"Is the answer in inches?"

"Is the answer in feet?"

"Is the answer in yards?"

Just dowse the appropriate number and start digging.

Distance Dowsing

If you can dowse a specific location, what's to stop you from dowsing a specific description of that location?

Nothing.

In my work for Find Me the authorities often want a physical description of the missing person's location in addition to the GPS coordinates. Physical descriptions of the suspects involved in the case are also requested. Getting that description requires just another application of the yes/no technique.

Is the suspect male? Female?

Is the suspect a blond? A brunette? A redhead? Bald?

Does the subject have a tattoo?

Is the suspect in a house?

Is the house made of brick?

Are the roofing tiles red?

Is there a swimming pool in the back yard?

You can go on to build up a complete and detailed description of the subject at hand just by asking basic questions.

THE PRACTICAL PENDULUM

Dowsing the Human Body

You can dowse existing or potential health trouble spots by dowsing your body (or someone else's body).

I was asked to help someone track down a trouble spot that was causing her physical pain and mental stress. She was someone I had never met and therefore had no experience with any sickness or injury she may have had. *She stretched out on a massage table and I held my hand over her body – not touching – and moved over her from head to toe while swinging my pendulum. I asked for a "yes" response whenever a trouble spot was encountered. Several locations generated "yes" responses. After the session she noted that she had been getting pains in those areas. I then dowsed the source of the pain.

"Is the pain due to muscle problems?"

"Is the pain due to skeletal problems?"

"Is the pain due to a strained ligament?"

"Is the pain due to current medication?"

"Is the pain psychosomatic?"

"Should she seek immediate medical attention?"

In such situations, I believe my job is only to point out potential trouble areas – not to diagnose or to provide medical or health advice. Following the session, I discouraged self-treatment based solely on dowsing and I strongly encouraged her to seek the advice and care of medical professionals.

Again, distance is irrelevant. The subject doesn't have to be in your physical presence for you to dowse potential health challenges. You can dowse your own ailments, or those of someone else, by using a representation of the human body, such as a drawing, a photograph or even a doll. Set clearly in your mind that the illustration represents the physical body of the subject and then just move a pointer over the body. Ask for a "yes" response when you come to any trouble spot.

If you get a "yes," make note of the exact spot. Don't stop. Other trouble spots may be encountered with further research.

Note: I could write additional chapters on dowsing the "health" of your car or truck, home heating and cooling system, computer or whatever. But the technique is the same regardless of the "health" need. Just follow the technique above for whatever system that "ails ya.'"

*For the record, I insisted that another female be in the room during this examination.

THE PRACTICAL PENDULUM

Dowsing the Future

I am not a strong believer in the theory that the future is set, that everything is pre-determined and there is nothing we can do about it.

However, I do believe it is possible to dowse likelihoods.

"Is it likely that I will get that promotion?"

"Is it likely that the missing person will be in Tucson tonight?"

"Is it likely that I will build a strong relationship with Ralph and Alice?"

I believe that the future is constantly changing according to every action we take. If your answer to the promotion question was yes and you then decide to celebrate by getting drunk at lunch, returning to work half-bagged, and getting up on a desk to shout, "I gotta' few things ta' say 'bout this crummy company." Well, chances are that your actions have dramatically altered the future you just dowsed.

Dowsing a likelihood can be informative and helpful. I worked a missing person case involving a young woman who had disappeared and was believed to be heading from the Midwest down to the Southwestern states. Dowsing indicated that the woman was hitchhiking along Interstate 40 and that she had been picked up by a traveling salesman. I estimated travel times and dowsed the likelihood of an end-of-the-day stop, getting a near 100 percent at Albuquerque. Additional pendulum work indicated that he would be stopping overnight at a specific motel. I also dowsed the likely name of the salesman.

I was curious about the accuracy of my work. I called up the motel and brought out my best good ol' boy accent and asked if my good buddy (using the dowsed name) had booked a room. The attendant glanced at her registration book and confirmed his scheduled late arrival for that evening. I turned the information over to the local authorities to let them take charge.

Whether or not the future is set, pendulum dowsing can help you and yours prepare for whatever likelihood may occur.

Using Your Body as a Pendulum

Your body can also be your pendulum.

Stand up erect and close your eyes. You'll notice a tendency to sway one way or another. That motion can be used to dowse information.

For example, let's assume you're lost in the desert. Stand up and close your eyes. Relax. Breathe slowly and easily and ask the question.

"Which way should I go to find the trail?"

"Which direction is north (south, east or west)?

"Should I stay here and wait for rescue?"

"Should I try to find my way out?"

As with a standard pendulum, a right swing will give you a *yes* answer and a left will give you a *no* answer.

Experiment with this technique. It's a fun exercise and I think you'll be surprised how accurate a technique it can be.

# Radiesthesia

Radiesthesia is the scientific term for pendulum dowsing.

It is a handy term for people whose egos can't handle saying, "I work with a rock on a string." I guess they prefer to amaze their friends at parties with, "I work in the field of radiesthesia" or "I'm a radiesthesiologist." Of course, that could lead to a response of, "That's great. Could you look at this bobo on my bum?"

I prefer to say, "I'm a pendulum dowser" and let the conversation go where it goes from there.

THE PRACTICAL PENDULUM

Stumbling Blocks

As with every human on the planet, you will have good days and bad days working with the pendulum. No one is 100 percent accurate 100 percent of the time and it is inevitable that you will have "on" days and "off" days. That's natural and to be expected. Generally, a psychic with a head cold is just not going to have a good day. If you're on medication, had a fight with your significant other, just bit your tongue or whatever, it will have an effect on your performance and your accuracy.

Sometimes you can work through the challenge. Other times, the best course is to hold off and come back to the problem at a later time.

Typical stumbling blocks are:

Lack of sleep

Lack of seriousness

Lack of faith in the process or in yourself

Pendulum obsession

Forgetting to check accuracy during the process

Illness

Overconfidence

Strong emotional response to the subject

Strong emotional influences (anger, sadness, and so on)

Closed mind

Alcohol or drugs

Medication

Mental problems

Listening to skeptics.

Asking poorly worded questions

Wishing for specific answers

Superstitions
Lack of concentration
Impatience
Fatigue
Distractions (traffic noise, kids next door, and so on)
Lack of motivation

What if I "Lose It" and Can No Longer Get Accurate Answers?

You can't lose something that is an essential part of what makes you you. It is possible to have ineffective readings, bad days or even slumps in performances. You're human and nobody performs at 100 percent capacity all the time.

If you're having a run of poor performances, take a break. Relax and realize that variations in the quality of performance are natural. Don't allow worry to influence your performance and cause the challenge to last even longer.

Trust the process. Trust yourself. You will inevitably find your way back.

Find Me

I am a co-founder of Find Me and have devoted the vast majority of my pendulum dowsing work to that organization and to the individual people, families and organizations we serve.

Find Me is a 501(c)3 non-profit organization of talented psychics, retired and active law enforcement officers, legal and investigative experts, working with a highly-trained search and rescue team. We have members from all over the world. We are a unique group. Since its inception Find Me has received more than 400 requests for help, and the number of requests are increasing. The Find Me network of 200 screened volunteers works collectively to locate missing persons and solve homicides.

The mission of FIND ME is to bring resolution and closure to families of missing persons. Whether it is children or adults who have been abducted, victims of homicide or other unexplained disappearances, Find Me is devoted to their families and seeks justice for the missing.

You can find out more on Find Me at the website www.findmegroup.org.

Exercises

1. Cover a photo so that you cannot tell what it represents. For example, flip to a page in a magazine and cover a photo with your hand or have someone select one for you and put it in an envelope or folder. Use your pendulum to determine what the photo represents.

Some sample questions: Is it an object? Is it a person? Is it bigger than a breadbox? Is it physically alive now? Is it in my kitchen? Is it electrical? Do I possess one?

2. Have someone hide something around the house or down at the neighborhood park and then try to find it. Remember to ask the question before the question: Did he/she hide something from me? Determining the size or other characteristics of the hidden object can help narrow down the search area. You can also apply map dowsing techniques by sketching out the floorplan of the house or area in which the object is hidden. "Build a box" and shrink it with targeted questions. Is it above doorknob level? Is it on the floor? Is it in something? Is it on something? Is it behind something? Is it hidden in plain sight?

3. Select an interesting case from your local media and work it as if you were assigned to solve the crime. Collect as many clues as you can in a case file and then follow the progress of the case in the news as a way of verifying your information.

4. Describe a place before going there. If you're going on a business trip or a vacation, use your pendulum to build up a description of the place you'll be going. Unlike solving a crime, which can take months or years to verify your information, you'll be able to verify your reading the moment you arrive. Note: This isn't predicting the future. The place already exists.

About the Author

Dan Baldwin is the author, co-author or ghostwriter of more than 50 books on business. He is also the author of the "as told to" book, *Find Me*, about the organization of that name, the *Caldera* series of Westerns, *Trapp Canyon*, and *Bock's Canyon*, Westerns, the *Ashley Hayes Mysteries*, the political thriller *Sparky and the King*, and the short story collection *Vampire Bimbos on Spring Break*.

Baldwin is a co-founder of Find Me, an international group of psychics, retired and active law enforcement personnel, legal and investigative experts, and search and rescue teams. He appears in the documentary *Pounding the Ground* about psychic detecting. Baldwin has earned numerous local, regional and national awards for writing and directing film and video projects; had earned the National Indie Excellence Awards Finalist designation for his Western Novels *Caldera III – A Man of Blood* and *Trapp Canyon*; his short story *Flat Busted* earned an honorable mention in the national Society of Southwestern Authors writing competition.

Baldwin can be contacted through his websites:
www.fourknightspress.com
www.danbaldwin.biz
baldco@msn.com.

Printed in Great Britain
by Amazon